HEROES OF AMERICAN HISTORY

THURGOOD MARSHALL

Sara Cucini

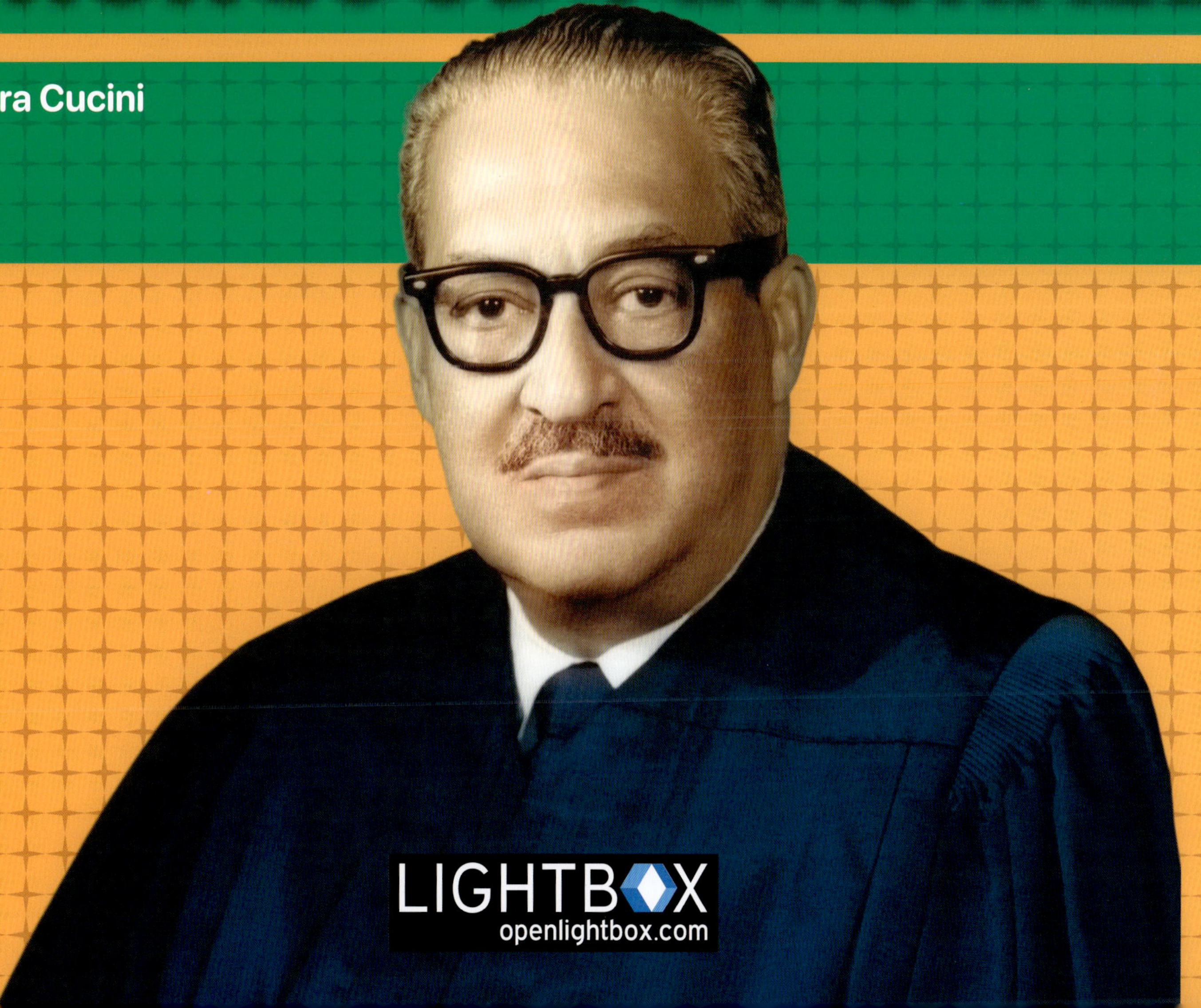

LIGHTBOX
openlightbox.com

LIGHTBOX

Go to
www.openlightbox.com
and enter this book's
unique code.

ACCESS CODE

LBXL6438

Lightbox is an all-inclusive digital solution for the teaching and learning of curriculum topics in an original, groundbreaking way.

OPTIMIZED FOR

- ✓ TABLETS
- ✓ SMART BOARDS
- ✓ COMPUTERS
- ✓ AND MUCH MORE!

STANDARD FEATURES OF LIGHTBOX

- **AUDIO** High-quality narration using text-to-speech system
- **VIDEOS** Embedded high-definition video clips
- **ACTIVITIES** Printable PDFs that can be emailed and graded
- **WEBLINKS** Curated links to external, child-safe resources
- **SLIDESHOWS** Pictorial overviews of key concepts
- **INTERACTIVE MAPS** Interactive maps and aerial satellite imagery
- **QUIZZES** Ten multiple choice questions that are automatically graded and emailed for teacher assessment
- **KEY WORDS** Matching key concepts to their definitions

SUPPLEMENTARY RESOURCES

- **SHARE** Share titles within your Learning Management System (LMS) or Library Circulation System
- **CURRICULUM** Find national and state curriculum correlations
- **CITATION** Create bibliographical references following APA, CMSO, and MLA styles

VIDEOS

WEBLINKS

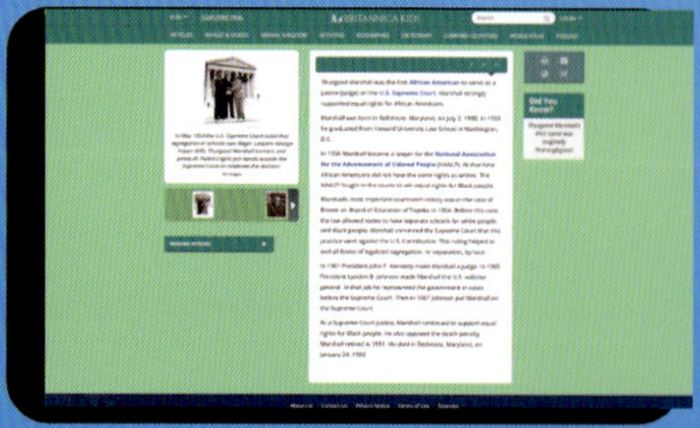

SLIDESHOWS

QUIZZES

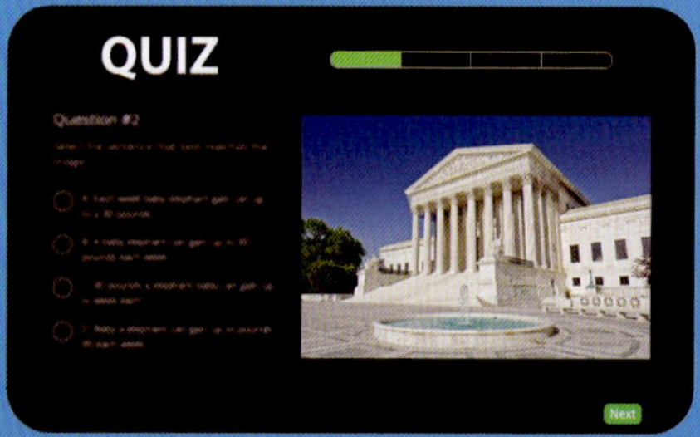

This title is part of our Lightbox digital subscription

1-Year Texas Subscription
978-1-5105-8659-8

Access hundreds of Lightbox titles with our digital subscription.
Sign up for a **FREE** subscription trial at **www.openlightbox.com/trial**

The digital components of this book are guaranteed to stay active for at least five years from the date of publication.

THURGOOD MARSHALL

CONTENTS

Who Was Thurgood Marshall?

Thurgood Marshall was a Supreme Court Justice. He worked to make Black Americans equal to White Americans under the law.

In 1967, Thurgood became the first Black American to join the U.S. Supreme Court.

Growing Up

Thurgood was born on July 2, 1908. His mother was a teacher. His father worked for the railroad. As a child, Thurgood was a good student. He loved to read.

Thurgood was born in Baltimore, Maryland.

Overcoming Obstacles

Thurgood wanted to be a lawyer. He was turned away from one law school because he was Black. Thurgood went to Howard University Law School instead.

UAW SAYS JOBS and FREEDOM FOR Every American
WE MARCH FOR FIRST CLASS CITIZENSHIP NOW!
WE DEMAND AN END TO BIAS NOW!
WE MARCH TOGETHER CATHOLIC JEWS PROTESTANT FOR DIGNITY AND BROTHERHOOD OF ALL MEN UNDER GOD NOW!
WE DEMAND AN END POLICE BRUTALITY NOW!
JOB EQUALITY FOR ALL MINORITIES
WE DEMAND EQUAL RIGHTS NOW!
WE DEMAND DECENT HOUSING NOW!
HOME RULE
HOME RULE
HOME RULE

Becoming a Lawyer

Thurgood believed that Black people should have the same rights as White people. As a lawyer, he fought to make this happen.

An Important Fight

In 1954, Thurgood won an important case. It allowed Black students to go to the same schools as White students.

Thurgood won 29 of the 32 cases he argued in front of the Supreme Court.

Thoughts from Thurgood

Thurgood wanted everyone to have a fair chance in life. He did not believe that skin color should hold people back.

"In recognizing the humanity of our fellow beings, we pay ourselves the highest tribute."

– Thurgood Marshall

Values

Thurgood was brave and determined. He was not afraid to fight for his beliefs. His courage helped change America's laws.

40
THURGOOD MARSHALL
UNITED STATES COURTHOUSE
ACCESSIBLE
ENTRANCE ON
PEARL STREET

Achievements and Successes

Thurgood was a Supreme Court Justice from 1967 to 1991. He helped many people. To honor Thurgood, people named buildings and streets after him.

In 1993, the president of the United States gave Thurgood a medal for the important work he had done.

Thurgood Marshall Timeline

1908
Born

1933
Graduates from law school

1954
Wins Black students the right to go to the same schools as White students

1965
Is named solicitor general, the top lawyer for the U.S. government

1967
Becomes the first Black American Supreme Court Justice

1991
Retires from the Supreme Court

1993
Dies at the age of 84

2022
Congress votes to place a statue of Thurgood in the U.S. Capitol.

Cause and Effect

Cause

Thurgood fought for equal rights among Black and White Americans.

Effect

Laws were changed to give Black Americans equal rights.

Cause

Thurgood was a good lawyer who won most of his cases.

Effect

He became the first Black American to serve on the U.S. Supreme Court.

SIGHT WORDS

Research has shown that as much as 65 percent of all written material published in English is made up of 300 words. These 300 words cannot be taught using pictures or learned by sounding them out. They must be recognized by sight. This book contains 59 common sight words to help young readers improve their reading fluency and comprehension. This book also teaches young readers several important content words, such as proper nouns. These words are paired with pictures to aid in learning and improve understanding.

Page	Sight Words First Appearance
4	a, Americans, first, he, in, make, the, to, under, was, White, who
7	as, child, father, for, good, his, mother, on, read, up
8	away, be, because, from, one, school, turned, went
11	have, people, rights, same, should, that, this
12	an, go, important, it, of, same
15	back, beings, did, life, not, our, thoughts, we
17	and, change
19	after, had, him, many, states, work

Page	Content Words First Appearance
4	law, Supreme Court Justice, Thurgood Marshall, U.S. Supreme Court
7	Baltimore, July, Maryland, railroad, student, teacher
8	Howard University Law School, lawyer, obstacles
12	case, fight
15	chance, humanity, skin color, tribute
17	beliefs, courage, values
19	achievements, buildings, medal, president, streets, successes, United States

Published by Lightbox Learning Inc.
276 5th Avenue, Suite 704 #917
New York, NY 10001
Website: www.openlightbox.com

Library of Congress Control Number: 2025937848

ISBN 978-1-5105-8257-6 (hardcover)
ISBN 978-1-5105-8258-3 (static multi-user eBook)
ISBN 978-1-5105-8260-6 (interactive multi-user eBook)

Printed in Guangzhou, China
1 2 3 4 5 6 7 8 9 0 29 28 27 26 25

062025
110824

Project Coordinator: Heather Kissock
Designer: Terry Paulhus
Layout: Jean Faye Rodriguez